JOSEPH CROMPTON:
A JOURNEY OF FAITH

JOSEPH CROMPTON:
A JOURNEY OF FAITH

Nicholas Groves

PAUL DICKSON BOOKS

JOSEPH CROMPTON:
A JOURNEY OF FAITH

published by Paul Dickson Books, May 2022

Paul Dickson Books, 156 Southwell Road, Norwich NR1 3RP,
t. 01603 666011,
e. paul@pauldicksonbooks.co.uk,
www.pauldicksonbooks.co.uk

ISBN 978-1-7397154-0-3

A CIP catologue record for this booklet is available from the British Library
Designed by Brendan Rallison
Printed in Norfolk by Cheverton Printers

CONTENTS

ILLUSTRATIONS

PREFACE

I first encountered Joseph Crompton when researching for my doctoral thesis, which was on the Ritualist churches of Norwich. The church of St Lawrence was an early (indeed, the second) convert to the Ritualist cause in Norwich, and Crompton became its Rector after a very turbulent period which involved the notorious 'Father Ignatius' (Joseph Leycester Lyne). Looking into his background, I found that he had started out as minister of the Octagon Unitarian Chapel, and thought at the time that that was a remarkable change of views. It was not until forced idleness over the summer of 2020 gave me the opportunity that I was able to look further into his life. What I was not to know in 2008 was that I should mirror his journey in reverse, going from St George Tombland, another of the churches which had a Ritualist tradition, to the Octagon. In my case, organ-playing was the catalyst.

What the members of the Octagon thought of the goings-on at St Lawrence we can but guess; likewise we can only guess (though probably with some degree of accuracy) what St Lawrence's thought of the Octagon. It takes a degree of fortitude for someone to change their religious views so much, but to do so in the same city, as a clergyman, even more so. That Joseph Crompton came out of this with goodwill on all sides says much about him.

NWG
Norwich
October 2021

1. A UNITARIAN BACKGROUND (1813-52)

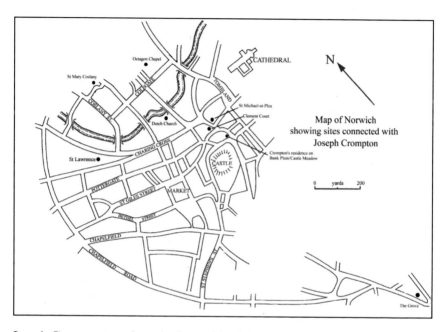

Map of Norwich showing sites connected with Joseph Crompton

Joseph Crompton was born in the parish of St Martin, Birmingham on 29 June 1813, the fifth child of seven of John William Crompton and Martha *née* Webster,[1] and baptized twenty-three months later, on 15 May 1815, at the Unitarian New Meeting House.[2] The New Meeting at that date was in Moor Street, having moved there in 1726 from the original 1692 Lower Meeting House. In 1862, it relocated to the neo-Gothic Church of the Messiah in Broad Street (where members of the Martineau family were among the members, and one of Crompton's sisters, Susan, married the minister, George Dawson), and finally, in 1973, to Ryland Street, resuming its former name of New Meeting.

The Moor Street chapel was burnt down in the 1791 riots against Joseph Priestley, the minister from 1780 to 1791; it was rebuilt, and re-opened in 1803. When the

---

[1] Pigot's *Directory* for Birmingham for 1841 lists him simply as 'merchant', at 6 Temple Row. This indicates a solid middle-class background.

[2] Copy of baptismal certificate in his Church of England ordination papers, NRO, DN/ORD 36. The baptism must have included some kind of formula acceptable to the authorities, as he was not required to undergo a conditional baptism.

congregation moved in 1862, it was sold to the Roman Catholics, who turned it into St Michael's Church, which is still functioning.

It is not known where Crompton received his early education, but a passing mention in Henry Solly's book *These Eighty Years* refers to 'our old friend Joseph Crompton (formerly my fellow-student at the London University)'.[3] At that date, this refers to what is now University College London (UCL), which adopted the name 'London University' when it was founded in 1828, taking its current name when it became one of the two founding colleges of the University of London when that was chartered in 1836. It was set up as a secular college, with no religious tests at all, nor even a chapel (prompting the Anglican counterblast of King's College in 1829), and was disparagingly referred to as 'the godless institution of Gower Street'. It was therefore popular with nonconformists, although it could not award degrees until the federal University was chartered in 1836. The *Calendar* for 1831 shows that Crompton spent the sessions 1828-29 and 1829-30 there, studying classics,[4] completing the Senior Division in both Latin and Greek. The fact that he was fifteen when he started suggests that this was in preparation for a university career, and is also an interesting sidelight on who was attending this new institution.

Nonconformists were, at this time, unable to graduate at Oxford or Cambridge, as to do so required subscribing to the formularies of the Church of England,[5] so many of them took their degree at one of the Scottish universities, which of course made no such stipulation, or occasionally a Dutch one. Crompton therefore attended the University of Glasgow, and graduated MA in 1834, aged 21.[6]

---

3 H Solly, *These Eighty Years, or, the story of an unfinished life*, Cambridge, 1893, p 311. Henry Solly (1813-1903) was a Unitarian minister at Yeovil. He was much involved in the foundation of institutions such as Working Men's Club Institute Union, the Charity Organization Society, and in 1884 devised a scheme of 'industrial villages' which prefigured the later Garden City movement. One of Crompton's brothers, William Morgan Crompton, married an Anne Solly. The University *Calendar* shows only an Isaac Solly as contemporary.

4 *The London University Calendar for the Year MDCCCXXXI*, p 193 ff.

5 Oxford required this on matriculation, so was never an option; Cambridge did not require it until graduation, so it was possible to follow the course but not to graduate. This requirement was abolished by the Oxford University Act of 1854 (but for the BA only), and the Cambridge University Act of 1856 (for all degrees except those in Divinity). Durham also changed its regulations in 1865 along the same lines. The Universities Tests Act of 1871 did away with all religious tests, and allowed not only nonconformists and Roman Catholics but also Jews and other non-Christians to hold professorships, fellowships, etc, as well as to graduate, without declaring that they were *bona fide* members of the Church of England. A failed attempt to abolish the oaths in 1834 was one of the direct causes of the foundation of the University of London, which has never imposed religious tests.

6 https://www.universitystory.gla.ac.uk/biography/?id=WH10252&type=P [accessed 21 November 2020] The MA, a four-year course, is a first degree at the 'ancient' Scottish universities (St Andrews, Glasgow, Aberdeen, and Edinburgh – and also Dundee, a daughter of St Andrews, chartered in 1967).

Admitted as a Unitarian minister in 1837, Crompton had a charge for two years at Frenchay Common, Bristol, and was then called to the Octagon Chapel, Norwich, in 1839, where he stayed until 1852. The Martineau family form the link between Norwich and Birmingham: two of them were among those who invited Crompton to the Norwich charge.[7] Originally a Huguenot family, they descended from Gaston Martineau, a surgeon who came to Norwich as a refugee from the revocation of the Edict of Nantes in 1686. The family were originally members of the French Church,[8] but, as with many of the other families, by the fourth generation had gradually drifted away: many became members of the Octagon, though some joined the Church of England. More importantly, some of them moved to Leeds and Birmingham where they became merchants, and as we have seen, they attended the New Meeting. As Crompton's father was a member, and also a merchant, family links did the rest.

The 1841 census records him as resident in the parish of St Michael-at-Plea.[9] The handwriting of the enumerator is so poor it is difficult to work out the exact address, but it seems to read Castle Meadow. If so, this would be one of the houses now under the southern end of the 1927 rebuild of Gurney's Bank,[10] on the corner of Bank Plain and Castle Meadow: White's 1845 *Directory* gives his address as Bank Plain, which might imply it was the corner house. The house was shared with three other young men, all annuitants, with two female servants. In the adjacent house was James Mottram, a bank clerk, and his family: the Mottrams were prominent members of the Octagon.[11]

Colegate, where the chapel is situated, was at that time one of those nexuses of religious activity that happen in towns like Norwich. As well as the Octagon, the

---

[7] C Binfield, 'Church and Chapel' in C Rawcliffe and R Wilson (eds), *Norwich Since 1550*, Hambledon & London, 2004, p 422. James Martineau's influence on the chapel was great, even though he had moved away: he recommended two of Crompton's successors, JD Hirst Smyth (1862) and Alexander Gordon (1872).

[8] This met in the former parish church of St Mary-the-Less in Queen Street. The congregation had dwindled so much by 1832 that the church was let out to other denominations – first the Swedenborgians, and then from 1852 until 1953 to the Catholic Apostolic Church.

[9] The transcript has him as 'Jos Crampton'.

[10] Lately 'Open'.

[11] An association dating back to the congregation's foundation (indeed, a Mottram was one of the original trustees), and only brought to an end with the death of Sophia Hankinson (*née* Mottram) in 2019.

Congregational Old Meeting House was next door,[12] while across the street was St Clement's Particular Baptist chapel,[13] all three sandwiched between the parish churches of St Clement-at-Fyebridge, at that time an evangelical stronghold under Richard Rigg, and the old-fashioned non-party St George Colegate; St Miles Coslany, at the far end of the street, was also under Mr Rigg's care. Just round the corner were St Mary's Particular Baptists,[14] and also St Mary Coslany, where Crompton was to serve from 1872-74. Sunday mornings on the street must have been interesting!

The chapel itself at this date was still much as Dr John Taylor[15] had conceived of it in 1756: it had its *scagliola* columns and 'tub' pulpit, and the body of the chapel was filled with box-pews, though an organ had been installed in the north gallery behind the pulpit in 1802.[16]

---

[12] The congregation dates from 1643; they built their Meeting House in 1693. It became 'Old' when the Presbyterians next door rebuilt their 1689 meeting-house as the Octagon in 1756: initially that was called the New Meeting House. The parish boundary between St Clement and St George runs along the wall dividing the two chapels, the Old Meeting being in St Clement's parish and the Octagon in St George's.

[13] Built 1814 for Mark Wilkes when he was ejected from Tabernacle. Thomas Archibald Wheeler became minister in 1844, leaving in 1864, then returning in 1870; it was known as 'Wheeler's Chapel'. The congregation moved to a new chapel on Unthank Road in 1875, when the General Baptists from Priory Yard took St Clement's over; they closed it in 1910 and amalgamated with the congregation on Silver Road. A significant amount of the chapel, without its façade, still stands.

[14] Zoar Strict and Particular Baptist, which is across the street from St Mary's (and ultimately formed from a schism from it), was not founded until 1886.

[15] John Taylor (1694-1761, minister of the Presbyterian congregation 1733-57. The original meeting-house, a domestic-style building opened in 1689 which stood to the west of the Octagon, was in such a bad way that it was decided to build a completely new chapel. The octagonal form was most likely Taylor's idea and not (as has often been asserted) Thomas Ivory's, though Ivory did a good deal of work in building the chapel: see V Nierop-Reading, *Two Classical Nonconformist Chapels in Norwich*.

[16] The pillars were first re-painted (terra-cotta), and the pulpit rebuilt in rostrum style, in 1889, when the organ was also enlarged. It was the first organ to be installed in a nonconformist chapel in Norwich, other chapels not doing so until about sixty or more years later. St George Colegate had gained one in the same year: which was first?

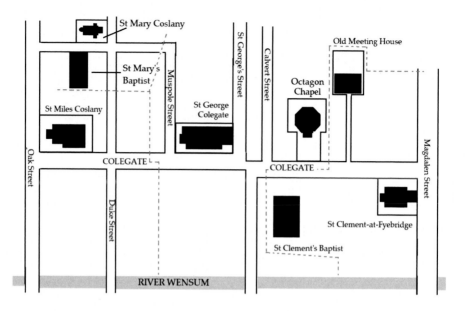

Diagrammatic map to show the various religious buildings in and around Colegate in 1839. The grey dotted lines indicate roughly how the parish boundaries run; the river forms the southern boundary.

Unitarian doctrine (if indeed one may call it that) at this date is not easy to define exactly, but it was still recognizable as a form of Christianity – if unorthodox (or heretical, depending on one's viewpoint).[17] The legal use of the name 'Unitarian' had only been made possible in 1813[18] (the year of Crompton's birth). The chapel had, until then, been described as Presbyterian, which is where it had started as a congregation as early as 1669. The congregation had, however, moved towards definitely Unitarian views under Thomas Madge (minister 1811-25), although John Taylor (minister 1733-57, and rebuilder of the chapel) had published works

---

[17] The emergence of Unitarianism as a distinct body is chronicled in Valerie Smith's book *Rational Dissenters in Eighteenth-century England*, particularly chapter 3. Put very simply, Rational Dissent rejected the concepts of the Trinity and of Original Sin, though basing these positions on interpretation of the scriptures. In this they differed from both the Church of England and 'Orthodox Dissent' – Congregationalists, Baptists, Methodists, etc.

[18] This was made possible by the 'Trinity' Act, largely piloted through Parliament by William Smith, the radical MP for Norwich and committed Unitarian. He was also instrumental in the repeals of the 'Test' and 'Corporation' Acts, and was grandfather of Florence Nightingale and Barbara Bodichon, one of the founders of Girton College. However, the term was in use before that date: Thomas Drummond preached a sermon at Ipswich meeting-house, where he was minister, 'for the benefit of the Unitarian Charity Schools' in 1807 (*Bury & Norwich Post*, 18 February 1807): these were the schools established at Norwich under Joanna Scott's will. There was also a Unitarian Friendly Society in Norwich, established in 1824 (For these and other examples, see Smith, *Rational Dissenters*, p 180. She is wrong in saying that Drummond established the schools.)

attacking the doctrine of Original Sin (see below), incurring the wrath of, among others, John Wesley.

The Octagon's heyday was 'the last decades of the eighteenth century and the first of the nineteenth ... It was the religious centre for the Norwich intelligentsia – families such as the Taylors, the Aldersons, and the Martineaus'.[19] Although the 'brilliant circle' died away, the intellectual tradition continued, but alongside one of social concern. The congregation maintained the Presbyterian School in King Street: Allcock's Yard on the corner near Rose Lane commemorated Trivett Allcock, its long-serving headmaster.[20] The school stood just north of it, fronting onto Rose Lane.[21] Those leaving the school were interviewed by members of the chapel committee, which demonstrates a degree of personal engagement. The Brotherly Society was founded in 1824 to visit and help the sick, though it was more than just that: it was a fraternal society, with officers rotating without regard to social class: 'at one time the chairman might be a Martineau: at another the local bricklayer'.[22] It also developed a brass band as an expression of unity and equality.

In 1843, Crompton published a sermon, *The Temperance movement considered in relation to the Christian Church – a sermon suggested by the visit of Father Mathew, delivered at the Octagon Chapel, Norwich, Sunday 10 September, 1843*. Theobald Mathew (1870-1856) was an Irish Roman Catholic priest and proponent of teetotalism. A member of the Capuchin order, he started his ministry in Cork, and quickly became associated with the temperance movement there. He preached widely in England, and also in the United States. The sermon is considered in Rob Donovan's doctoral thesis: Crompton argued that it was 'the deficiency of vitality ... due to concentration on doctrinal issues' that explained why there was now a need 'to reach the drunken and the abandoned'. Any claim that 'the advocation of the temperance societies are liable to the charge of excess

---

[19] R Hale, 'Nonconformity in Nineteenth Century Norwich' in C Barringer (ed) *Norwich in the Nineteenth Century*, p 178. Most of what follows is from this source. There were two unrelated Taylor families at the chapel.

[20] The yard was at no 45 King Street, and is now under a housing complex next to the St John Ambulance HQ. Trivett Allcock (1789-1868), initially resident on the Horsefair, had moved to Tombland in 1851, the year he married Elizabeth Southgate, a widow; the Probate register says he died in Heigham.

[21] The boys' school had moved by 1885 to a site immediately north of the Octagon. The girls and infants were further north still, near Calvert Street Methodist chapel, all now under that end of the flyover. I am grateful to Trevor Nuthall for this information. The boy's school was merged in 1910 with the King Edward VI Middle School and the Municipal Higher Grade School to become the City of Norwich School, at Eaton.

[22] Hale, *ibid*.

in their language and proposals' was but 'a natural effect of a reaction against an evil which has been allowed to increase almost to a state requiring divine retribution'. At such a time, '…(the) priest of Rome, members of the Church of England, and dissenters, are all one … because then we are all truly Christian'.[23] Donovan goes on to remark:

> There is a feeling of being almost overwhelmed by an evil that required in response a renewed recognition of common Christian identity. The evil is presented as drink but was this rather the 'presenting problem'? The 'Drink Question' is more a symptom of the underlying structural problem of a society in economic transition and at the same time coping with a revolution in ideas that seemed to threaten religious certainties.[24]

Another of Crompton's sisters, Martha (1806-72) married Edward Utting Dowson of Geldeston in 1840; his brother, John Withers Dowson, was very involved at the Octagon.[25] It seems likely that she came to Norwich with Joseph, possibly to keep house for him, and found her husband through the chapel. Joseph did not marry for another eleven years: on 9 September 1851, his last year at the Octagon, he married Sarah Hayward.[26] She was fourteen years younger than him, being born (at Melton in Suffolk, on the edge of Woodbridge) in 1827, but at the time of their marriage she was living with Ann Gardiner, her unmarried aunt, at Newmarket Terrace, and was probably a member of the chapel.[27] They had no children.

Joseph and Sarah Crompton lived on Bracondale, in a house called The Grove, which occupies the triangular plot between Bracondale and King Street.[28] The site is large, comprising four acres, 'with two houses and plantation, garden, and pleasure ground'.[29] The property belonged to WF Paul, and was conveyed to JJ

---

23 From the sermon: quoted in R Donovan, *Drink in Victorian Norwich*, unpublished PhD thesis, UEA, 2003, p 270. (The sermon is held at the Norwich Heritage Centre, C252).

24 Donovan, *ibid*, p 271.

25 The families connected with the chapel form highly complicated intermarried networks: through his brother-in-law Edward Utting Dowson, Crompton was connected with two previous ministers, William Enfield (in post 1785-97) and Pendlebury Houghton (in post 1787-1806 and 1810-12).

26 *Norwich Mercury*, 13 September 1851.

27 1851 Census. Next-door but two was JJ Colman of the mustard dynasty. The Colmans, originally Baptists, had become Congregationalists. The 1841 Census also shows her at that address.

28 Contemporary sources always give the address as just 'Bracondale'. *Norfolk Annals*, in the note of his death, gives his address as The Wilderness, which is the house at the other end of Bracondale, at the top of Carrow Hill, until recently known as Carrow Hill Hostel. It is unclear when the houses on The Grove were built, but they are Victorian.

29 Unilever-archives.com – reference BR61/3/7/1-2, abstract of title to The Grove in Bracondale. Given Crompton's interest in the sciences and education, it is good to record that, in the years before its closure in 1993, the smaller boys of Bracondale School were regularly taken to The Grove for nature classes.

Colman in 1860. It drops steeply from both roads, as it was a mediæval chalk-extraction pit, later used as a public garden.[30]

Fig 1: Interior of the Octagon Chapel in 1848, drawn from the west side of the gallery. Image from J and E Taylor's history of the chapel.

It is not known exactly when Crompton took up residence at The Grove: the Religious Census of 31 March 1851 (where he is listed as minister of the Octagon: interestingly even this late he was described as 'Presbyterian (Unitarian)') gives his address as Magdalen Street:[31] possibly he had moved there from his rooms on Bank Plain ready for when he married in September that year. However, we may assume he moved to Bracondale in 1852 – the Microscopical Society was founded

---

[30] http://www.heritage.norfolk.gov.uk/record-details?MNF61562-Medieval-chalk-extraction-pit-Bracondale-Grove&Index=53405&RecordCount=54877&SessionID=98112152-2524-49e1-86b4-c708562748c4 [accessed 11 January 2012]

[31] The Ancestry transcription of the main 1851 Census, taken the day before the religious one, has him listed as 'Crantton', and his place of birth as 'Bemmingham', which does not assist in finding him! The house was on the west side of Magdalen Street, north of the junction with Colegate: as no house numbers are given it is hard to work out quite which property is intended, but might it have been number 24, which had been owned by the Martineaus? He had two servants.

8

in that year at his house, which would fit better than rooms on Bank Plain – and he was certainly there by 1854, as White's *Directory* for that year has his address as 'Bracondale'. The Census of 1861 records him there, with Samuel Harvard, the chief accountant at Colman's mustard mill, in the other house. The 1871 Census describes him as 'Landowner, Dissenting Minister, Free Church in Dutch Church'; he had a cook and a housemaid. The other house was still occupied by Mr Harvard. In 1872, he was recorded as resident in Bracondale when the declaration of *Si quis* was read at Trowse Church.[32]

Crompton's ministry was

> characterised by a breadth and liberality ...[which] in course of time became so pronounced and so firmly established that, when requested to 'openly to promulgate those doctrines which distinguish Unitarians from other Christians, and to instruct his hearers in the scriptural grounds of their faith', he preferred to resign rather than give the weight of his office to any creed which might be fettering to any of the Church members – holding that 'each was bound to have and know his own opinion, while there should be no creed fettering the Church, nor any authority of priesthood, ministry, or deacons, to enforce any form of belief'.[33]

This view is far more in tune with present-day Unitarianism, although he was working within a basic Christian framework. It is not known when or why he was requested to 'promulgate those doctrines'. In 1896, the Octagon Chapel was ejected from Norwich's Free Christian Union when it changed its name to the Evangelical Union, specifically so that the Octagon could be removed from membership, as it was not regarded by the other nonconformist churches as truly Christian. However, this was well after Crompton had left the Octagon (and indeed was dead), so it cannot have been then. Presumably it was while he was still at the Octagon, and not a Free Christian.

---

[32] NRO, DN/ORD 36. The *Si quis* ('If anyone ...') is a notification by a candidate for Holy Orders of his intention to enquire whether any impediment may be alleged against him, somewhat like banns of marriage. Most of Bracondale lies within the ecclesiastical parish of St Andrew, Trowse: the boundary now runs between nos 13 and 15, so it went through the middle of the former Bracondale School.

[33] Obituary, *Norwich Mercury*, 24 April 1878.

2. THE FREE CHRISTIANS (1852-74)

Crompton 'grew to dislike the definitively Unitarian theology of the congregation, and desired to revive the less dogmatic theology of an earlier period.'[34] In his Introduction to *The History of the Octagon Chapel, Norwich*,[35] he divided the chapel's history into three phases:

1. 'the old orthodox doctrines';
2. 'mostly Arian';
3. Unitarian.

When it started life as a Presbyterian congregation, there is no doubt that the doctrines were those of mainstream nonconformist Christianity, and Peter Finch (minister 1691-1753) used the Scottish Assembly's Catechism. But Crompton goes on to say that the Presbyterians, alone among the denominations, were 'always free in doctrine and discipline – all others having creeds or articles fixed in books, title-deeds, or enforced by some other method'.[36] Thus the Presbyterians were not exclusive, and members would speak only for themselves individually, and not for the church as a whole: 'a form of Christianity free from dogmatism'. The Presbyterians, he said, had

> performed the office of giving shelter and religious union to those liberal and enlightened minds of their time who, having thrown off the domination of Popery in Rome, found no rest in the priestcraft of the Church of England, or the disguised Popery of Dissenting orthodoxy.[37]

Their chapels were always open to all, as opposed to the Congregationalists, who required a conversion experience before full membership was granted.

---

34 Anon, *The Octagon Chapel, Norwich*, Norwich; no date. His predecessor, John Taylor, had disclaimed all names for the congregation beyond 'Christian' (see below).

35 Taylor, J and E, *The History of the Octagon Chapel, Norwich*; London, 1848, p iii. (Hereafter *HOC*.) Crompton wrote the seven-page Introduction, in which a good deal of his theology is set out.

36 *HOC*, p iii. Scottish Presbyterianism, with its firm Calvinist basis, is a very different thing from the English version. It was the latter's openness to variety of belief that led most if not all Presbyterian congregations into Unitarianism. Trinity Presbyterian (now URC) in Norwich was founded by four Scottish linen-drapers in 1866, erecting the first chapel, on Theatre Street, in 1875. It moved to Unthank Road (on the site of a former Baptist chapel) after the original chapel was bombed in 1942.

37 *HOC*, p iv.

Under Dr John Taylor, the Octagon moved towards Arianism,[38] and he certainly eschewed any denominational title for the congregation: in his sermon at the opening of the new chapel in 1756, he said 'We are *Christians*, and only *Christians*, a name which in its original and true meaning includes all that is virtuous and amiable ...'.[39] Again, in this period the Octagon provided 'a point of union for men of various shades of dogmatic belief'.[40]

However, Crompton saw Unitarianism as having become 'dogmatic rather than spiritual in its manifestations', and he lamented that

> The fundamental idea of its system is the pure and perfect one of seeking for the facts and uncontroverted truths of religion as the centre of union for all forms and shades of church and doctrine. That popular exposition of belief which has vulgarly received the name of the 'Apostle's Creed' contains nearly all the principles adopted into that theology, and around it all the faith and feeling in devotion is left to be wound by the individual conscience of everyone for himself.[41]

It was his view that Unitarianism had become, in the popular view, 'a system of negations', but that the Octagon Chapel was 'not a Unitarian chapel in the common antagonistic sense of the term. The congregation is free.'[42] He believed that 'the time is come to cease from destructive action, and to trust in the swelling power of truth, and to labour constructively. The people want bread of life, not Athanasian, Arian, or Unitarian disquisitions.'[43] But this was the *zeitgeist:*

> The age ... was a controversial and dogmatic one; logical lucidness and systematic controversy, more than spiritual fire, was the characteristic of the time, and of some of the leaders of the body.[44]

Put another way, he wanted a religion of the heart, not of the head.

---

[38] Put briefly, this is the doctrine that the Son, while divine, is not eternal, but was created by the Father, and is therefore not God by nature but by creation, and is subordinate to the Father. It was at various times up until the fourth century the official form of Christianity, and can be supported from scripture, but was eventually declared to be a heresy in favour of Trinitarianism at the First Council of Nicæa in 321 CE.

[39] *HOC*, p v. Legally, however, it remained Presbyterian.

[40] *HOC*, p vi. See also GT Eddy, *Dr Taylor of Norwich: Wesley's arch-heretic*; Epworth Press, 2003. Taylor rose to prominence in 1740 with his book *The Scripture Doctrine of Original Sin*, a devasting attack on that doctrine. John Wesley was among those who opposed him.

[41] *HOC*, p vii.

[42] *HOC*, p viii.

[43] *HOC*, p viii.

[44] *HOC*, p vii.

He therefore resigned his charge in 1852, and with several former members of the Octagon[45] he founded a denomination called the 'Free Christians'.[46] Initially, they met in the old Library Hall, over the porch of St Andrew's Hall. This had been rebuilt in 1774 to house the City Library, and was also used as a courtroom (see Fig 2). It was taken down and replaced with the current flint-faced one in 1863.

Fig 2: St Andrew's Hall with the 1774 porch. The hexagonal tower had fallen in 1712 and was replaced by the bell-cote, itself now gone. Image courtesy of Norfolk County Council at www.picturenorfolk.gov.uk.

In 1852, when the porch room became too small, they moved to a room in Clement Court, which had started life as a ball-room belonging to two dancing-masters; first, John Boseley, and then Francis Christian and his son. It was also used for assemblies. From 1832 to 1852 it was used by the Catholic Apostolic Church, and when they moved to St Mary-the-Less across the street Crompton took it on. After he left in 1858, it was used by the Plymouth Brethren. The room ended its life as the Public Health Laboratory. It was demolished in the 1950s.

---

[45] Including the last-surviving Martineau at the Octagon, Frances Anne – see below. Binfield, 'Church and Chapel', p 422.

[46] Hibgame, *Recollections of Norwich...*, p 31, says it was called the 'Reformed Church of England', but that denomination was not formed until the 1870s (N Yates, *Anglican Ritualism in Victorian Britain, 1830-1910*, OUP 1999 p 207). Crompton's organization had no connexion with the Free Christians currently linked with the Unitarians, or indeed with any other organization at all, so far as can be made out. The congregation's records are preserved in the Norfolk Record Office.

In September 1858 Crompton asked the Corporation if, when the Guardians of the Workhouse surrendered the lease on the Dutch Church, it could be assigned to the Free Christians.[47] This was the chancel of the Blackfriars' church, given to the Dutch-speaking congregation, originally 'Strangers', for worship. As with the French Church, they had largely been integrated by about 1800 and attended the various other churches and chapels (by 1851 there was just a single service in Dutch held once a year), so they no longer needed their own chapel. From 1805 to 1858, it was used as the Workhouse chapel, the workhouse being in the old Blackfriars' buildings: a new one was built on the Bowthorpe Road in 1858,[48] so the building was again vacant.

After some delay, the lease was granted to Crompton on 20 October 1858, on condition that he undertook to repair the building. This he did, and the chapel was re-opened for worship on Sunday 12 February, 1860, with services at 11:00 and 18:30. The renovations included removing the brickwork that had been intruded into the lower parts of the windows, unblocking the east window (which had been completely bricked up),[49] and repairing the floor. The old pulpit was replaced by a new one; new, open benches were installed for seating, enough to seat five hundred; and a single-manual organ by Mark Noble was bought.[50] So far as is known, no images of the interior of the building when fitted up as a chapel survive, but we may assume it followed the standard nonconformist layout with a central, elevated, pulpit, and the communion table beneath it.[51] This all suggests that the congregation was large enough and financially secure enough to fund all this, but exactly how numerically strong the Free Christians were is not clear: it is unfortunate that the Religious Census took place in 1851, just before the church was set up, so we have no idea of the numbers attending,

---

[47] *Norwich Mercury*, 25 September 1858.

[48] It became the West Norwich Hospital.

[49] The tracery design is that of the original window, though it was largely rebuilt in 1959.

[50] *Bury Free Press*, 18 February 1860. The alterations were 'under the superintendence of Mr C Darkins'. This was most likely the builder Canuel Jabez Darkins, whose daughter Susannah married TA Wheeler of St Clement's Baptist. He had been a member of Rehoboth Particular Baptist chapel, which stood in Union Place, though it had shut in 1833; doubtless he had joined Wheeler's chapel. His first given name, though it sounds like a minor Old Testament character, is a two-syllable surname: his paternal grandfather spelt it Cannewll. The organ went to Horsham St Faith in 1894, and then to Horsford in 1973. It was rebuilt there in 1993.

[51] After Crompton left, it was used from 1878 to 1888 by a congregation of Primitive Methodists, who called themselves the Primitive Gospel Band. There was a proposal to turn it into a school in 1886, so the remainder of the two-hundred-year lease was purchased from the Dutch congregation, and presented to the Corporation, who then took the building over, it reverting absolutely to their possession in 1913 when the lease expired, at which point they had control of both parts of the building.

but it does record that on Census day, 31 March, the Octagon attracted 250 at the morning service, with a further 247 'Sunday scholars', and 136 in the evening.[52]

DUTCH CHURCH

ST. ANDREWS HALL, NORWICH.

The Restoration of this Edifice being completed, it will be RE-OPENED, for Divine Worship, by the

REV. JOSEPH CROMPTON, M.A.,

On SUNDAY, the 12th of FEBRUARY.

Divine Service at Eleven in the Morning, and Half-Past Six in the Evening.

A COLLECTION AFTER EACH SERVICE.

Entrance by St. Andrew's Hall Garden and Elm Hill.

Fig 3: Advertisement from the Norwich Mercury announcing the reopening of the Dutch Church

The Free Christians held an enormously popular social event every year, open to non-members. In July 1853 it was held 'on Miss Martineau's beautiful grounds at Bracondale',[53] when four hundred guests enjoyed refreshments 'under a handsomely decorated marquee, which, during the late hours of the evening, was tastefully illuminated'; a brass band played, and the church's choir sang anthems and glees.[54] The following year, again at Miss Martineau's, it attracted six hundred,

---

[52] ed J Ede and N Virgoe, *Religious Worship in Norfolk: the 1851 Census of Accommodation and Attendance at Worship*, Norfolk Record Society, vol LXII, 1998, p 124. Thomas Wheeler noted in his entry for St Clement's Chapel that Census day was wet, and that this affected the numbers attending. He recorded 380 in the morning and 263 in the evening; the Old Meeting attracted 442 and 437 respectively.

[53] This was Bracondale Lodge (or Hall). The site was acquired by Philip Meadows Martineau (1752-1829) in 1793; he built the house in 1795, with a garden landscaped by Humphrey Repton. It was demolished in 1960, and the site is now occupied by County Hall; the link is preserved by the street-name Martineau Lane if that section of the ring road that passes it. Martineau also purchased Carrow Abbey in 1811, later acquired by the Colmans. Miss Martineau was Philip's unmarried daughter, Frances Anne (1812-77), apparently known in the family as 'Fanny Annie'. As noted above, she was the last-surviving member of the family at the Octagon, and joined the Free Christians when they were formed.

[54] *Norfolk News*, 23 July 1853.

14

and 'comprised, we were glad to observe, persons of various denominations, amongst whom were many belonging to the Octagon Chapel, of which the Rev J Crompton was formerly the pastor'.[55] In 1856, the *Norfolk News* noted that

Fig 4: The exterior of the Dutch Church (Blackfriars' Hall).
Author's photograph.

Once every year Miss Martineau's beautiful grounds at Bracondale are the scene of such a mingling of sects and parties as is witnessed, so far as we know, nowhere else in

[55] *Norfolk News*, 5 August 1854.

this county. The precise reason for this we cannot exactly determine. Other religious denominations besides the Free Christians have their annual tea parties and social gatherings, and like that church refuse tickets of admission to no respectable persons who may choose to make application, and yet we remember no similar occasion on which so many and such diversified religious creeds are represented as that the yearly assemblage on Miss Martineau's grounds, under the auspices of the Free Christian Church. It is not our business to speculate on the causes which contribute to this: we have simply to record the fact and express our gratification at the evidence this evinced of the possibility of inducing the various religious sects sometimes to forget their differences and to meet on terms of the warmest and most cordial sympathy and friendship ... ... Amongst the mottoes, the most significant one was 'unity of spirit in diversity of opinion'.[56]

These were large-scale events, not just in terms of attendance: the 1856 account says that the afternoon was spent in 'various sports', followed by tea at six o'clock in the marquee, and then more sports until half past eight, when everyone reassembled in the (now illuminated) marquee for addresses, and 'the company separated shortly after ten o'clock'. It was still at Miss Martineau's in 1858, but an account of the 1861 meeting records that it was held 'on the grounds of the Rev J Crompton at Bracondale',57 and that 200 sat down to tea; they were later regaled with an account of Crompton's tour in Italy.

The Norwich Free Christians seem to have died away following Crompton's ordination into the Church of England: some of them joined the Church of England with him;[58] others could not bring themselves to do so: possibly they joined other nonconformist denominations; maybe some returned to the Octagon, but (so far as is known) there was no attempt made to continue the congregation.

---

56 *Norfolk News*, 19 July 1856. The 'mottoes' were inscriptions, probably decorating the marquee.

57 *Norfolk News*, 17 August 1861. However, a note at the end says the JJ Colman was thanked 'for the use of his meadow'. As Miss Martineau did not die until 1877, it is unclear why the venue shifted.

58 *Bury & Norwich Post*, 13 January 1874.

3. THE CHURCH OF ENGLAND AND ST LAWRENCE (1874-78)

During the twenty-two years he ran his Free Christian congregation, Crompton gradually moved toward a mainstream Trinitarian theology. His views eventually 'approximated to those of the Broad Church party',[59] he said that he was 'a Dissenter against his will', and that the sole stumbling-block to his joining the Church of England was the Athanasian Creed.[60] He 'wrote letters to the public press ... with a view to reforming the liturgy particularly in reference to the Athanasian Creed'.[61]

The Athanasian Creed (or *Quicunque vult;* 'whosoever will be [saved]', from its opening words) is a long, very abstruse, text setting out the doctrine of the Trinity.[62] By law, it was recited during Morning Prayer on a number of saints' days, and also on Christmas Day, and Easter Day, and Trinity Sunday – about once a month on average, though not always on a Sunday. It was the focus of a debate in the late 1860s and early 1870s, with some clergy (basically, those of the Broad Church party, but also some evangelicals) wanting its use discontinued, while others defended it.[63] The focus of the discontent was the 'damnatory clauses' at the start:

> Whosoever will be saved: before all things it is necessary that he hold the Catholick Faith. Which faith except everyone do keep whole and undefiled: without doubt he shall perish everlastingly.

and at the end:

> This is the Catholick Faith: which except a man believe faithfully, he cannot be saved.

---

[59] 'Broad Church' at this date referred to those members of the Church of England who accepted a more liberal theology, such as not accepting the literal truth of the Bible, and who, on the whole, accepted the findings of Darwin and Buckland, but it covered a very wide variety of opinion. They were opposed on two sides, by the Evangelicals and the Ritualists (Anglo-Catholics), as well as by the 'old-fashioned orthodox', all of whom took a conservative stance on doctrine and scripture.

[60] *Norfolk Chronicle*, 22 April 1878.

[61] *Norfolk Chronicle*, 27 April 1878. There were many attempts to make the Prayer-Book more comprehensive, and acceptable to Nonconformists at this time, but all were rejected. One such of 1852, in my possession, was generally believed to have been compiled by the Prince Consort and the Chevalier Bunsen, but was in fact the work of Henry Hunt Piper, a Unitarian minister.

[62] It can be found in the 1662 Book of Common Prayer following Evening Prayer – 'At Morning Prayer', or in the 1928 one as '*Quicunque vult*'.

[63] See further on the debate Joshua Bennett, 'The age of Athanasius: the Church of England and the Athanasian Creed, 1870-1873' in *Church History and Religious Culture*, 97 (2), from which much of what follows is taken.

It had been proved by the mid-nineteenth century that it was not written by Athansius (296-373 CE), but probably dates from the late fifth or sixth century, and was most likely composed in southern Gaul. It was not used liturgically by any other Western church, though it is accepted by most of them;[64] the Eastern churches did not, and still do not, accept it at all. Various suggestions were mooted, such as changing 'shall' into 'may be' in the rubric ordering its use, or cutting out the damnatory clauses, as well as abandoning its use altogether. Ultimately, when the Church of England's Convocation debated the matter in 1872, it voted to retain its use as ordered. It gradually faded into obscurity, particularly after its use was made optional by the unapproved, but widely-used, Prayer Book of 1928. It is still included in the current service books, *Common Worship*, though it merely notes (on p 143) that 'the authorized form of the Athanasian Creed is that contained in the Book of Common Prayer' and does not provide a text, much less a modernized version. Presumably what Crompton had objected to was the damnatory clauses.

Quite what prompted this step is somewhat unclear, especially given his statement above that 'there should be no creed fettering the Church, nor any authority of priesthood, ministry, or deacons, to enforce any form of belief', and that he had spoken slightingly of 'the priestcraft of the Church of England'. People's views do change, but this does seem to be a particularly major one.

He was ordained into the Church of England at his own request: he was deaconed on 20 December 1874 by the Bishop of Norwich, John Thomas Pelham, and priested the following year.[65] Quite what preparation he was required to undertake is not known: ordination requirements at this date were set by the individual bishops. His Glasgow MA was very unlikely to be acceptable alongside the more usual Oxford and Cambridge ones: despite the greater length and rigour of the Scottish degree, the few holders of them who were ordained in the Church of England were usually regarded as literates – *i.e.*, non-graduates: perhaps that is why he used his postnominals whenever he could! This had to do with the fact that the Scottish universities operated in a different way and had a different curriculum from the English ones, and were under the control of the Presbyterian church.[66]

---

[64] In the Roman Catholic Church it was recited as part of the office of Prime on some Sundays, which was usually recited by the clergy alone in any case (and in Latin), so the Church of England was innovative in introducing it as part of public worship in 1549.

[65] There was a report in several papers that he would 'probably take orders in the diocese of Exeter' (*e.g. York Herald*, 9 January 1874.) It is not clear where this idea came from.

[66] Sara Slinn, *The Education of the English Clergy 1780-1839* (Boydell, 2017), p 109. As she notes, the favour was returned, with the Scottish church not thinking very highly of Oxford and Cambridge degrees!

John Thomas Pelham, Bishop of Norwich 1857-93, was a decidedly evangelical cleric, a change from the three liberal bishops of the previous fifty years, all of whom had looked kindly on nonconformists. Pelham would not ordain non-graduates as a rule, and he was also opposed to the idea of theological colleges. So most likely Crompton's ministerial work was taken into consideration, and he was a 'known quantity' in the city, so probably he was merely required to undergo a formal examination. Crompton was supported, as required, by testimonials from three beneficed clergy: Jonathan Bates, Rector of Kirstead; George Harris Cooke, Vicar of Worstead; and Charles Baldwin, Vicar of St Stephen's.[67]

Fig 5: John Thomas Pelham, Bishop of Norwich 1857-93.
Image courtesy of Norfolk County Council at www.picturenorfolk.gov.uk.

---

[67] NRO, DN/ORD 36. Baldwin was a signatory to a letter to the *Norfolk Chronicle* of 2 July 1864 which 'earnestly and affectionately' entreated Edwin Hillyard to dissociate himself from JL Lyne (see below). Cooke became Vicar of St Helen in 1891; his brother, William Harris Cooke, was the very popular Rector of St Saviour, 1856-1909, the church invaded by JL Lyne after he left St Lawrence. One of his churchwardens for many years was AM Stevens, a prominent member of the Octagon Chapel (*Eastern Daily Press*, 18 August 1898). Bates' career was wide-ranging, but a possible link maybe that he was 'one of the Examiners for the Society of Arts': if he examined at the Peoples' College (see below) that may explain how he knew Crompton (see *Crockford's*, 1874).

The next day, Crompton was licensed as curate to Charles Morse, Rector of St Michael-at-Plea and of St Mary Coslany.[68] Morse held these two livings in plurality (St Michael 1839-86, St Mary 1851-82), but at that time was unable to carry out his duties because he was incapacitated as a result of the Thorpe Railway Accident.[69] Crompton stayed there for two years, and 'galvanized the churches into life'.[70] This did not last, however, for when Thomas Lord visited St Michael on the afternoon 15 June 1884, he noted

> This venerable old church seems now neglected, as the Sunday previous there was no Congregation for the Minister to preach to – even this day my son Ralph and myself alone comprised the congregation (excepting the Sexton's two children) one of which rung the Church bell prior to service. I informed the Sexton that I did not wish the service to go on solely for me – though I must confess I realised the novelty somewhat.[71]

Lord says that the Rector was now 'too infirm' to take service, and on this occasion the officiating cleric was a J Beard.[72] As there was no clerk, Lord read what he calls the clerk's part' of the service – *i.e.*, the congregation's part, which had come to be recited by the clerk alone. Mr Beard preached nonetheless: 'a dry, somewhat un-sympathetic discourse' – and it was read and not preached not extempore, Lord much preferring the latter.

In 1876 Crompton was appointed to the Rectory of St Lawrence in Norwich: 'a few friends with a number of the parishioners solicited that it might be conferred

---

[68] Diocesan Curates' Licences (NRO, DN/CUR/18). The 1877 edition of *Crockford's* inaccurately says Crompton was curate from 1872. Morse was born in Norwich in 1805, and died in 1886. In 1874, he was living with his family in Calvert Street.

[69] *Norfolk Chronicle*, 27 April 1878. This occurred on 10 September 1874, when two trains were involved in a head-on collision on the single-track line between Norwich and Brundall. The up-train, a mail-train, should have been held to allow the down-train, the London-Yarmouth express, a clear run. Owing to late running, and a series of administrative errors, this did not happen, and the two trains collided at Thorpe. Both of the drivers and firemen were killed, along with seventeen passengers; another fourteen died of injuries later. Seventy-three more were seriously injured: Morse was one such; he was sixty-nine at the time. It resulted in the introduction of the tablet system.

[70] *DS*, 17 March 1900.

[71] NRO MC 1619/1. Thomas Lord made it his business to visit every church and chapel in Norwich for a service over the course about eighteen months, and record what he found: external and internal appearance of the church, and notes on the way the service was conducted. Although he said he would record 'without prejudice', it is clear that he had absolutely no sympathy for the new high church customs.

[72] I have no idea who he was. Neither the edition of Crockford for 1874 nor for 1885 lists a Beard in Norwich, and the only J Beard was resident in Wolverhampton. As he turns up again, officiating in the Rector's absence when Lord went to St Lawrence on 24 August 1884, I think we can assume that he did not get the man's name wrong. It is just possible that he was a Reader: the office had been revived in 1866.

upon him'.[73] It is the third-largest of the surviving churches of Norwich,[74] and is situated between St Benedict's Street and Westwick Street. The ground slopes so steeply towards the river that its south side is below ground-level, but the north side is some three metres above it.

The church was emerging from a very turbulent period under its previous Rector, Edwin Hillyard (1861-76), who, in addition to adopting the most advanced Ritualist practices in the services, had also allowed the *soi-disant* 'Father Ignatius' (the deacon Joseph Leycester Lyne) and his 'monks' to play a prominent part in them: it was most probably Lyne who persuaded Hillyard to introduce the full ritual practices, including the use of incense. It was the second church in Norwich to adopt Ritualism, and, while this was unpopular in the first place, the presence of Lyne's adherents made it worse. The church lost its resident parishioners as worshippers,[75] and gained a new eclectic congregation who liked that style of worship – many from St Gregory Pottergate, which had been the first church to adopt this style, but was now in retrenchment under a new Vicar who was undoing all the ceremonial advances. The parish called a meeting in May 1864 to discuss 'the special services held every morning at 7 o'clock in that church which were a great nuisance to the parish':[76] they were so theatrical that many people came for the show, and not to worship; they took about two hours. Lyne quarrelled with Hillyard in 1866, and the 'monastery' came to an end in that year; Lyne eventually moved to Llanthony.[77]

In the meantime, Lyne had been trying to get Hillyard to remove the box-pews, and hence their rents (which formed a considerable addition to the Rector's stipend), but to no avail, as Hillyard did not wish to antagonize the congregation. So one night in 1865, Lyne and his supporters entered the church and chopped

---

[73] *Norwich Mercury*, 24 April 1878. The living is in the gift of the Lord Chancellor.

[74] St Peter Mancroft is the largest, and St Andrew the next. The church's other claim to fame is that it is where Sarah Glover (1786-1867) developed her Norwich Sol-fa, later developed into Tonic Sol-fa by John Curwen. She had left Norwich in 1851.

[75] The 1851 Religious Census records 156 at the afternoon service that day – service alternating between morning and afternoon week by week. There were sittings for 500, which was possibly greater than the population of the parish.

[76] Account in *Norfolk Chronicle*, 14 May 1864.

[77] For a good account of Lyne, see A Calder-Marshall, *The Enthusiast*, Faber, 1962. The 'monastery' premises were on Elm Hill, where the entrance can still be seen, marked by a green plaque, next-door to number 14. The chapel also still stands to the side of the car-park behind: it is now used by Norwich University of the Arts, which calls it 'The Monastery'.

up the pews – utterly illegally. The loss of the pew-rents put a strain on the parish finances. The parish could not afford to re-seat the church with pew-benches until 1891 – and that may well have been at the expense of the then Rector – so they had to make do with rush-seated chairs until then.

Hillyard had several disputes with the authorities, as he continued with his 'advanced' services, and in 1867 the Bishop refused to licence an assistant curate to the parish. He left Norwich for Christ Church, Belper, in Derbyshire in 1876, taking with him a community of nuns he had founded in the parish. He was obviously fearful of what would happen to the Ritualist tradition on his departure, as in his parting address, he advised the congregation to abandon the church, and attend either St John Maddermarket or St Peter Hungate, both churches which by then had an established Ritualist use, though nowhere near so advanced.[78] This appears to have happened, as the church went into a decline.[79] The resident parishioners did not return, while those who had come from outside went elsewhere.

Fig 6: Edwin Hillyard, Rector of St Lawrence 1861-76.
Image courtesy of Norfolk County Council at www.picturenorfolk.gov.uk.

---

[78] *Norfolk C§*, 25 March 1876.

[79] *NDS*, 29 December 1897.

Fig 7a: Exterior of St Lawrence from the north-east (author's photograph)

Fig 7b: Exterior of St Lawrence from the south-east (author's photograph)
The extreme slope can be seen at the east end.

This was the church inherited by Crompton, and according to one obituary, he devoted himself to 'win back to their parish church those parishioners who had been alienated by the excessive ritualism' of Hillyard.[80] Clearly he was well-known in Norwich, and the request by parishioners as well as friends that he be given the living suggests that they thought he would be the ideal person to de-escalate the situation. Whether this would have happened we cannot know, for, as we shall see, he died just two years after his appointment. His lack of party-spirit was recognized by the fact that clergy of all schools – 'High, Low, and Broad' – attended his funeral.

Certainly he greatly toned down the ceremonial and adopted a simpler form,[81] and he had spoken against Ritualism at the great Protestant meeting called by the churchwardens of St John Maddermarket in 1873.[82] But this seems not to have worked: as noted, once Hillyard left, the church entered a decline which was only halted, and then only in part, when it was united with its neighbour, St Gregory Pottergate, in 1903. This is borne out by his obituary in *Eastern Daily Press* for 23 April 1878:

> A more striking contrast could hardly be conceived between those two rectors [Hillyard and Crompton]. Mr Crompton did his utmost to win the regard and confidence of his new flock, but, owing to their Ritualistic preferences, only partially succeeded. The change was in one sense too great. Every one, whether concurring or not in the reverend gentleman's views from time to time, gave Mr Crompton credit for honesty of purpose and the most excellent intentions.

Thomas Lord visited the church on the morning of 24 August 1884, but did not remark on the size of the congregation, though he noted that there was a choir of four men and ten boys – and that the mysterious Mr Beard officiated on that occasion also, in the Rector's absence.[83]

---

[80] *Norfolk Chronicle*, 27 April 1878. The great weakness of differing forms of worship, particularly in a multi-churched city, is that many people cease to attend their parish church, and attend one where the services are to their taste. Equally, the resident parishioners may find themselves alienated, which is what happened at St Lawrence. As noted above, Hillyard, with a fine disregard of the parochial system, advised his gathered congregation to abandon St Lawrence when he left and go to other churches of a like nature.

[81] 'A gorgeous ritualism was replaced by a simpler form of service, and the old congregation drifted away' (*DS*, 17 March 1900).

[82] Supplement to the *Norfolk Chronicle*, 26 April 1873. This meeting was to oppose the growing number of Ritualist clergy being appointed in the city: Maddermarket, hitherto an evangelical stronghold, had had one appointed in 1872, despite assurances by the patrons (New College, Oxford), that this would not happen, and it went on to become 'possibly the highest church in Norwich'. It closed in 1981.

[83] NRO, MC 1619/1, p 88.

An 'Account of Restoration' of the church up to 1930, held in the parish documents,[84] noted that about 1900, 'the worshippers could have been accommodated in one of the vestries', and that the building was in such bad repair it was thought to be redundant; it was 'left derelict by its parishioners who, save for marriages and funerals, seldom entered it'. The church was finally closed in 1968. It now stands empty, stripped of its furnishings, and cared for by the Churches Conservation Trust: the fact that the only access is via fifteen steps from the street-level to the nave floor makes its re-use problematic.

---

[84] NRO, PD 58/40

4. OTHER INTERESTS

Crompton was greatly interested in the natural sciences. He was a member of the British Association for the Advancement of Science, and acted as one of three local secretaries for its thirty-eighth meeting, held in Norwich during August and September 1868. He was associated with the Norfolk and Norwich Museum as a lecturer, alongside Professors Lindley[85] and Sedgwick,[86] and he lectured on several scientific topics around the county – 'Storms', 'New Facts in Astronomy, or, What the Stars are Made of', as well as one at Bungay on 2 March 1859 on 'France and the French'.

He was also a founding member of the Norfolk and Norwich Naturalists' Society, serving as President for its first two years (1869-71). The foundation of the NNNS was a direct result of the British Association for the Advancement of Science meeting held at Norwich in 1868.[87] It was also a successor to the Norwich Microscopical Society, which had been founded in 1852 at Crompton's house. The first meeting of the NNNS was held on 30 March 1869 at the Norwich Museum, and Crompton was elected President. A letter from JD Hooker to Charles Darwin ends:

> A queer man – Crompton of Norwich, is too modest to send you the enclosed, & asks me to do so – please tear it up – I do not want it again.[88]

Crompton's social conscience found expression in a number of ways. He sat on the committee of the People's College in Colegate, along with the Rev'd John Alexander of Princes Street Congregational Chapel, and his neighbours The Rev'ds Andrew

---

[85] John Lindley (1799-1865). Born at Catton, where his father was a nurseryman, he moved to London and became a botanist. He was assistant Secretary of the Royal Horticultural Society 1822-62, and Professor of Botany at University College, London, 1829-60.

[86] Adam Sedgwick (1785-1873), a founder of modern geology, though he opposed Darwin's (whom he taught) theory of natural selection. He was an Anglican clergyman, and was Professor of Geology at Cambridge 1818-73, and Vice-Master of Trinity 1844-62. He was a residentiary canon of Norwich Cathedral from 1834 to 1873, though he spent most of his time in Cambridge.

[87] KB Clarke, 'A Survey of the History of the Norfolk and Norwich Naturalists' Society' in *Transactions of the Norfolk and Norwich Naturalists' Society*, vol 22, part 4, 1972, p223.

[88] Letter, JD Hooker to Darwin, 7 March 1870, transcribed in *The Correspondence of Charles Darwin:* Volume 18, 1870, (Cambridge, 2010), p58, where it is suggested that the enclosure, which has not survived (so presumably Darwin did indeed 'tear it up') may have been Crompton's first presidential address to the Norfolk and Norwich Naturalists' Society, delivered on 27 April 1869. Hooker's uncle by marriage, John Gunn, was a member of the NNNS.

Reed of the Old Meeting House and Thomas Wheeler of St Clement's Baptist, and John Withers Dowson,[89] JH Gurney, and others.[90] The College was founded around 1850 by Edward Lombe,[91] with 500 students, and was intended

> to provide a good education for male and female adults of the working class at the lowest practicable charge, the course to be wholly unsectarian and free from party politics.[92]

An advertisement of 1850 stated that no fewer than fifty-eight classes were offered.[93] Instruction was provided in 'reading, writing, arithmetic, grammar, geography, drawing, etc', with language and mathematical classes available for an extra fee.[94] Lombe lost over £1000 in the venture, although it did not ruin him. It underwent a period of uncertainty following his death in 1852, but was restarted, and administered by a board consisting of a President, four Vice-Presidents, and a Council of eighteen, of whom six were to be drawn from the adult students.[95] It is not clear at present where the premises were, beyond being in that part of Colegate that is in St George's parish, nor when it finally ceased.[96]

Crompton served also as a Trustee of The Norwich Permanent Building Society, in Queen Street, along with John Withers Dowson and the Revd John Hallett,[97] and also as a Director of the Norwich Equitable Fire Assurance Company.[98]

---

[89] Dowson (1800-79) was a prominent member of the Octagon Chapel, being superintendent of the Sunday Schools from 1822 to 1870. His brother married Crompton's sister, so there was a familial link: see family tree on p 23.

[90] *Mason's General and Commercial Norwich Directory and Handbook,* 1852.

[91] Edward Lombe, ?1800-1852. This would be Edward Lombe of Great Melton, not Edward Lombe (*né* Beevor) of Bylaugh. He was a descendant of Sir Thomas Lombe, who had smuggled silk-weaving equipment into England from Italy in the early 1700s, thus freeing the country from dependence on the Italian weavers. Edward had an estate in Norfolk which brought in over £15,000 a year, so he was well able to bear the loss of £1000. He was an advocate of educational reform. He blamed the aristocrats, the Church, and 'those great pests, the dissenters' for the collapse of the college, so it is interesting that it was the latter who revived it. D de Giustino, *Conquest of Mind: Phrenology and Victorian Social Thought,* p 212 ff.

[92] Aims stated in *Norfolk Chronicle,* 16 October 1852.

[93] *Norfolk News,* 19 January 1850. New classes in political economy and chemistry were announced.

[94] *Norfolk News,* 8 November 1851. The fees for 1851 were a shilling a month, or half-a-crown for a quarter, payable in advance; the language and maths classes each cost 6d a term extra, or 1/3 for a quarter.

[95] There was also a day school for children.

[96] The Diocesan Training College moved to St George's Plain in 1853, but that had bought and adapted two houses specially; the site of those buildings is under the western end of what is now Jane Austen College, and was in St Miles' parish in any case. If it was still going by then, the Peoples' College appears to have had nothing to do with the Cambridge University Extension lectures, which started in 1877 (Colman, HC: *University Extension Lectures in Norwich, Diamond Jubilee,* 1877-1937).

[97] *Norwich Mercury,* 22 February 1871.

[98] AD Bayne, *A Comprehensive History of Norwich.*

Politically, Crompton was 'a decided Liberal'.[99] He was involved locally with parliamentary reform, especially concerned with widening suffrage. This led to 'friction between the Whigs and the more Radical section' of the local party,[100] and on 7 February 1859 'some of the more advanced Liberals formed themselves into a Committee of Independent Reformers'. It was chaired by Jeremiah James Colman,[101] and included, besides Crompton, JH Tillett, John Copeman, jr, Thomas Hamer, Josiah Fletcher, John Withers Dowson, Thomas Jarrold, JD Smith, the Rev'd George Gould, 'and others'. It passed a resolution that 'the Ministerial Reform Bill is an insult to the intelligence of the nation, and utterly unworthy of the support of any who profess to be reformers'.[102] The Reform Act of 1832 had extended the franchise to the middle classes, but this Bill, presented by Disraeli in February 1859, still did not extend the franchise to the working-classes: this did not happen until 1867, after a long and strenuous campaign.

In 1872, Crompton was involved in a political court case. Put briefly,[103] Robert Hardiment was accused of bribing voters to vote for Sir Henry Stracey at the previous General Election: he was found guilty at the Assizes in 1875, but as the crime was so serious, his sentence was reserved to the Court of Queen's Bench. Some associates were also charged; one was acquitted, another found guilty but also had his sentence reserved. Stracey's son, Edward, was also charged, but was found not guilty. Joseph Stanley, a solicitor, was also charged with conspiring with Hardiment and the others to bribe voters to vote for certain candidates in the municipal election of 1869. Hardiment was found guilty and sentenced to six months in prison, but Stanley was acquitted.

Crompton then seems to have brought a private prosecution against Stanley, who was tried before the magistrates in February 1875 and committed for trial at the Assizes. Stanley applied for a summons against Crompton, who, Stanley alleged, shook his fist in his face during an adjournment, and wanted Crompton to be bound over: 'He looked more like a fiend than a man. He was grinding his teeth

---

99   *Norfolk Chronicle*, 22 April 1878.

100   This information from HC Colman, Jeremiah James Colman, p 204.

101   Jeremiah James Colman (1830-98), a member of the mustard dynasty. He was initially a member of St Mary's Particular Baptist Chapel, but in the 1870s moved to become a member of Princes Street Congregational Chapel, where Dr GS Barrett was the minister.

102   HC Colman, *ibid*, p 205.

103   This account is from that in C Mackie, *Norfolk Annals*, vol 2, p 239.

and was perfectly white'.[104] Crompton denied it, giving an entirely different view, but he appears to have annoyed the bench by refusing to cross-examine Stanley (he was conducting his own case), but wanting to call witnesses, which was not permitted unless he did cross-examine; it is unclear why he would not. He was bound over for £10 on his own recogizance to keep the peace for three months. An attempt by his counsel, Mr Simms Reeve, an hour later to get the case reheard was denied.

Possibly this illustrates what the writer of his obituary had in mind when he said

> But if on some occasions his desire to do right took a Quixotic rather than a practical turn, and his own thoroughness and honesty of purpose rendered him too often the catspaw of others, with different aims and objects, his memory will not be less respected on that score. Both publicly and privately kindness of heart and unostentatious open handed charity won for him the affectionate regard of a very wide circle of friends and acquaintances, nor could even a great domestic affliction for some years past, or the privation occasioned by defective eyesight, quench the genial spirit of the man.[105]

---

104 Account of the hearing in *Norwich Mercury*, 12 February 1875.

105 *Norfolk Chronicle*, 22 April 1878. It is not known what the 'great domestic affliction' was.

5. DEATH

Crompton's time at St Lawrence was short: he died of pulmonary problems on Easter Monday, 22 April 1878, at The Grove. The obituary in the *Norfolk Chronicle & Norwich Gazette*[106] says that he had officiated at St Lawrence 'so recently as Good Friday last' (19 April) although suffering from pulmonary symptoms:

> in one less earnest and persistent in the performance of his public duties might have been well deemed an excuse for not risking exposure to the recent inclement winds.

The upshot was that he caught a severe cold which resulted in inflammation of the lungs 'with other complications', and this proved fatal. If he had walked to the church, and thus exposed himself to the wind, the most direct route from The Grove to St Lawrence is just over a mile; even if he drove, the church was most likely unheated at that date in any case.

The funeral 'of this much-lamented clergyman'[107] took place at St Lawrence on Thursday 26 April; the *Norwich Mercury* noted that 'in consequence of his being so widely known and so universally esteemed, it partook of a semi-public character'; all the shops in the parish were closed.[108] The first part of the service, by request of the parishioners, took place at St Lawrence. The church was crowded, and several private carriages were sent to represent their owners – among them those of the Mayor and Jeremiah James Colman.[109] Virtually all the city clergy were present, together with many prominent laymen, both Anglican and Nonconformist. The Rev'd James Wilson, the Vicar of St Stephen, officiated. The coffin was carried in to the Dead March from *Saul*, and then covered with a violet pall; Crompton's MA hood was placed on it by one of the churchwardens.[110] After the service, a cortège was formed, which passed along St Benedict's Street to the municipal cemetery in Earlham Road. St Lawrence's bells rang a muffled peal, while those of 'the neighbouring churches' were tolled,[111] and muffled peal was rung at St Peter Mancroft in the evening.

---

[106] 27 April, 1878

[107] Account of the funeral, *Norwich Mercury*, 27 April 1878.

[108] Ibid.

[109] Most of this information is from the account in *Norfolk Chronicle & Norwich Gazette* 27 April, 1878. The sending of an empty personal carriage to represent someone who could not attend was a standard practice at the time.

[110] A relative novelty, as Glasgow had not reintroduced academic hoods until 1868.

[111] This would be St Margaret-de-Westwick, St Swithin, and St Benedict, which the cortège passed, and possibly also St Gregory Pottergate and St Miles Coslany, which are close by.

The Probate Register shows that the Will was proved by Alfred Hayward, a merchant, of Woodbridge, and Edward Theodore Dowson, of Geldeston, his nephew.[112] He left a personal estate of 'under £14,000'. It is not clear what became of Mrs Crompton, but the *Norfolk Chronicle* of 8 June 1878 had an advertisement from Spelman the auctioneers that 'Furniture and effects from the late Residence of the Rev. J Crompton, deceased' would shortly be sold. She stayed in Norwich, as she died there on 22 March 1900.[113]

On 6 November 1879 a window in Crompton's memory was unveiled during evensong at St Lawrence by the Mayor, Harry Bullard. It is at the east end of the south aisle. The mainlights show a king, a bishop, a priest, and a deacon in their traditional vestments in the upper sections, with scenes from the parable of the Good Samaritan in the lower ones, with an inscription across the four lights, reading:

Beatus vir qui intelligit super egenum et pauperum in die mala liberabit eum Dominum
(Blessed is the man that considereth the poor and needy: the Lord shall deliver him in the time of trouble – Psalm 41:1)

The glass is by Clayton and Bell, with the stonework by Mr H Hammond of St Augustine's. The inscription across the base reads:
In memory of Joseph Crompton, MA, Rector of this parish, who died April 22nd 1878, aged 64.

A brass tablet is placed under it, reading:

'To the glory of God and in affectionate remembrance of the Rev Joseph Crompton, MA. Erected by public subscription as a mark of respect and esteem for his devotion to the poor and great interest in the welfare of the city – Harry Bullard, treasurer.'

---

112 This was his older sister Martha's son; a younger sister, Susan, slightly confusingly married George Dawson (see family tree on p 24). Hayward is most likely his wife's brother.

113 Her probate record gives no address other than 'of Norwich'.

Fig 8: The memorial window in St Lawrence. Image courtesy of Mike Dixon

TIMELINE

1813 – 29 June, born in Birmingham

1815 – 15 May, baptized at the New Meeting House

1828-30 – studying at London University

1839-34 – studying at Glasgow University

1834 – graduated MA at Glasgow

1837 – admitted minister; at Frenchay, Bristol

1839 – appointed minister of the Octagon Chapel, Norwich

1851 – 9 September: married Sarah Hayward at the Octagon

1852 – left Octagon and established the Free Christian Church

1852 – resident at The Grove

1852 – Norwich Microscopical Society founded at his house

1858 – obtained lease of Dutch Church

1860 – 12 February: re-opened Dutch Church after renovation

1869 – 31 March: elected first President of the Norfolk & Norwich Naturalists' Society

1874 – 20 December: ordained deacon in the Church of England

1874 – 21 December: licensed as curate to St Michael-at-Plea and St Mary Coslany

1875 – ordained priest in the Church of England

1876 – 7 November: instituted Rector of St Lawrence

1878 – 22 April: died

1878 – 26 April: funeral

1879 – 6 November: memorial window unveiled in St Lawrence

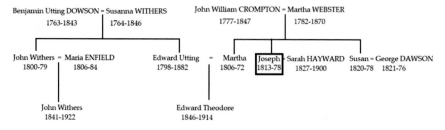

Tree to show relationship of Joseph Crompton with the Dowson family. Not all children are shown. Maria Enfield was a granddaughter of William Enfield, minister of the Octagon 1785-97.

BIBLIOGRAPHY

Manuscript sources
Norfolk Record Office (NRO)
DN/CUR/18 – curates' licences.
DN/ORD 36 – Crompton's C of E ordination papers.
MC 1619/1 – Thomas Lord's 'odyssey' round the churches and chapels.
PD 58/40 – St Lawrence's parish documents.

Printed primary sources
Ede, J and Virgoe, N (eds): *Religious Worship in Norfolk: the 1851 Census of Accommodation and Attendance at Worship*, Norfolk Record Society, vol LXII, 1998.
Mackie, C (ed): *Norfolk Annals: a chronological record of remarkable events in the nineteenth century (compiled from the files of the Norfolk Chronicle)*, Norwich, 1901, vol 2

Printed sources – books
The London University Calendar for the Year MDCCCXXXI, John Taylor, London, 1831.
Calder-Marshall, A: *The Enthusiast*, Faber, 1962
Colman, HC: *Jeremiah James Colman: a memoir*; London (privately printed) 1905.
Colman, HC: *University Extension Lectures in Norwich, Diamond Jubilee, 1877-1937*; Norwich University Extension Society, 1937.
Eddy, GT: *Dr Taylor of Norwich: Wesley's arch-heretic*; Epworth Press, 2003.
de Giustino, D: *Conquest of Mind: Phrenology and Victorian Social Thought*, London, 1975.
Smith, V: *Rational Dissenters in Late Eighteenth-century England*; Boydell, 2021.
Solly, H: *These Eighty Years, or, the story of an unfinished life*, CUP, 1893.
Taylor, J and E, *The History of the Octagon Chapel, Norwich*; London, 1848.

Printed sources – articles and chapters
Bennett, JMR: 'The age of Athanasius: the Church of England and the Athanasian Creed, 1870-1873' in *Church History and Religious Culture*, 97 (2), pp 220-247.
Binfield, C: 'Church and Chapel' in C Rawcliffe and R Wilson (eds), *Norwich Since 1550*, Hambledon & London, 2004, pp 409-435.
Clarke, KB: 'A Survey of the History of the Norfolk and Norwich Naturalists' Society' in *Transactions of the Norfolk and Norwich Naturalists' Society*, vol 22, part 4, 1972.

Hale, R, 'Nonconformity in Nineteenth Century Norwich' in Barringer C (ed) *Norwich in the Nineteenth Century,* Norwich, 1984, pp 176-197.

Theses

Donovan, R: *Drink in Victorian Norwich,* unpublished PhD thesis, East Anglia, 2003.

Groves, NW: *The Restoration of Popery': the impact of Ritualism on the Diocese of Norwich, 1857-1910, with special reference to the parishes of the City of Norwich and its suburbs;* unpublished PhD thesis, Lampeter, 2008.

Nierop-Reading, V: *Two Classical Nonconformist Chapels in Norwich;* unpublished MPhil thesis, Bath, 2002.

Local newspapers accessed via the British Newspaper Archive.

 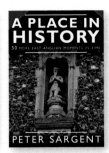 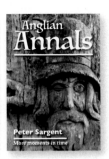 

PAUL DICKSON BOOKS
Books by Norfolk writers published in Norwich

Paul Dickson has lived and worked in Norfolk for the past 33 years, initially for the National Trust, then as an independent PR practitioner and latterly as an independent publisher and tour guide.

A meeting with Illuminée Nganemariya in 2006 saw Paul assisting with Miracle in Kigali, Illuminée's story of survival during the Genocide against the Tutsis in Rwanda and subsequent life in Norwich.

After a spell as a director of Norfolk's Tagman Press, Paul decided to branch out on his own in 2016. Since then he has embarked on collaborations with Norfolk writers, Tony Ashman, Janet Collingsworth, Sandra Derry, Nicholas Groves, Steven Foyster, Neil Haverson, Tim Lenton and Peter Sargent.

  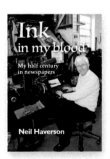 

www.pauldicksonbooks.co.uk